SCHIRMER PERFORMANCE EDITIONS

BEETHOVEN
PIANO SONATA No. 2
IN A MAJOR
Opus 2, No. 2

Edited and Recorded by Robert Taub

Also Available:
BEETHOVEN PIANO SONATAS
edited and recorded by Robert Taub

Volume I, Nos. 1–15
00296632 Book only
00296634 CDs only (5 disc set)

Volume II, Nos. 16–32
00296633 Book only
00296635 CDs only (5 disc set)

On the cover:
The Tree of Crows, 1822 (oil on canvas)
by Caspar David Friedrich
(1774–1840)
© Louvre, Paris, France/Giraudon/The Bridgeman Art Library

ISBN 978-1-4768-1610-4

G. SCHIRMER, *Inc.*

DISTRIBUTED BY

HAL•LEONARD®
CORPORATION
7777 W. BLUEMOUND RD. P.O. BOX 13819 MILWAUKEE, WI 53213

www.schirmer.com
www.halleonard.com

CONTENTS

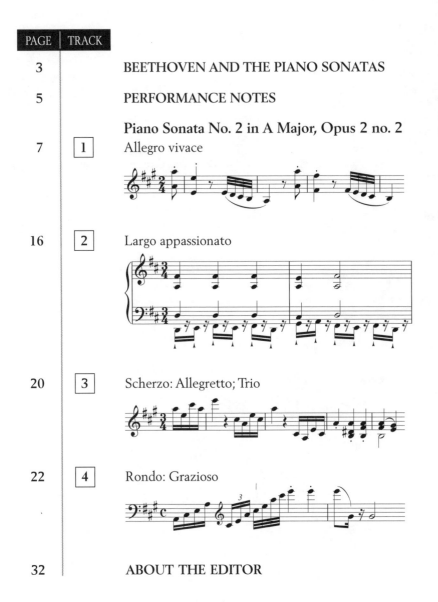

BEETHOVEN
AND THE PIANO SONATAS

In 1816, Beethoven wrote to his friend and admirer Carl Czerny: "You must forgive a composer who would rather hear his work just as he had written it, however beautifully you played it otherwise." Having lost patience with Czerny's excessive interpolations in the piano part of a performance of Beethoven's *Quintet for Piano and Winds*, Op. 16, Beethoven also addressed the envelope sarcastically to "Herr von Zerni, celebrated virtuoso." On all levels, Beethoven meant what he wrote.

As a composer who bridged the gulf between court and private patronage on one hand (the world of Bach, Handel, Haydn, and Mozart) and on the other hand earning a living based substantially on sales of printed works and/or public perform-ances (the world of Brahms), Beethoven was one of the first composers to become almost obsessively concerned with the accuracy of his published scores. He often bemoaned the seeming unending streams of mistakes. "Fehler—fehler!—Sie sind selbst ein einziger Fehler" ("Mistakes—mistakes!—You yourselves are a unique mistake") he wrote to the august publishing firm of Breitkopf und Härtel in 1811.

It is not surprising, therefore, that toward the end of his life Beethoven twice (1822 and again in 1825) begged his publishers C.F. Peters and Schott to bring out a comprehensive complete edition of his works over which Beethoven himself would have editorial control, and would thus be able to ensure accuracy in all dimensions—notes, pedaling and fingering, expressive notations (dynamics, slurs), and articulations, and even movement headings. This never happened.

Beethoven was also obsessive about his musical sketches that he kept with him throughout his mature life. Desk sketchbooks, pocket sketch-books: thousands of pages reveal his innermost compositional musings, his labored processes of creativity, the ideas that he abandoned, and the many others—often jumbled together—that he crafted through dint of extraordinary determi-nation, single-minded purpose, and the inspiration of genius into works that endure all exigencies of time and place. In the autograph scores that Beethoven then sent on to publishers, further layers of the creative processes abound. But even these scores might not be the final word in a particular work; there are instances in which Beethoven made textual changes, additions, or deletions by way of letters to publishers, corrections to proofs, and/or post-publication changes to first editions.

We can appreciate the unique qualities of the Beethoven piano sonatas on many different levels. Beethoven's own relationship with these works was fundamentally different from his relationship to his works of other genres. The early sonatas served as vehicles for the young Beethoven as both composer and pianist forging his path in Vienna, the musical capital of Europe at that time. Throughout his compositional lifetime, even when he no longer performed publicly as a pianist, Beethoven used his thirty-two piano sonatas as crucibles for all manner of musical ideas, many of which he later re-crafted—often in a distilled or more rarefied manner—in the sixteen string quartets and the nine symphonies.

The pianoforte was evolving at an enormous rate during the last years of the eighteenth century extending through the first several decades of the nineteenth. As a leading pianist and musical figure of his day, Beethoven was in the vanguard of this technological development. He was not content to confine his often explosive playing to the smaller sonorous capabilities of the instruments he had on hand; similarly, his compositions demanded more from the pianofortes of the day—greater depth of sonority, more subtle levels of keyboard finesse and control, and increased registral range.

These sonatas themselves pushed forward further development and technical innovation from the piano manufacturers.

Motivating many of the sonatas are elements of extraordinary—even revolutionary—musical experimentation extending into domains of form, harmonic development, use of the instrument, and demands placed upon the performer, the piano, and the audience. However, the evolution of these works is not a simple straight line.

I believe that the usual chronological groupings of "early," "middle," and "late" are too superficial for Beethoven's piano sonatas. Since he composed more piano sonatas than substantial works of any other single genre (except songs) and the period of composition of the piano sonatas extends virtually throughout Beethoven's entire creative life, I prefer chronological groupings derived from more specific biographical and stylistic considerations. I delve into greater depth on this and other aspects of the sonatas in my book *Playing the Beethoven Piano Sonatas* (Amadeus Press).

1795–1800: Sonatas Op. 2 no. 1, Op. 2 no. 2, Op. 2 no. 3, Op. 7, Op. 10 no. 1, Op. 10 no. 2, Op. 10 no. 3, Op. 13, Op. 14 no. 1, Op. 14 no. 2, Op. 22, Op. 49 no. 1, Op. 49 no. 2

1800–1802: Sonatas Op. 26, Op. 27 no. 1, Op. 27 no. 2, Op. 28, Op. 31 no. 1, Op. 31 no. 2, Op. 31 no. 3

1804: Sonatas Op. 53, Op. 54, Op. 57

1809: Sonatas Op. 78, Op. 79, Op. 81a

1816–1822: Sonatas Op. 90, Op. 101, Op. 106, Op. 109, Op. 110, Op. 111

From 1804 (post-Heiligenstadt) forward, there were no more multiple sonata opus numbers; each work was assigned its own opus. Beethoven no longer played in public, and his relationship with the sonatas changed subtly.

—*Robert Taub*

PERFORMANCE NOTES

Extracted from *Beethoven: Piano Sonatas Volume I*, edited by Robert Taub.

For the preparation of this edition, I have consulted autograph scores, first editions, and sketchbooks whenever possible. (Complete autograph scores of only twelve of the piano sonatas—plus the autograph of only the first movement of Sonata Op. 81a—have survived.) I have also read Beethoven's letters with particular attention to his many remarks concerning performances of his day and the lists of specific changes/corrections that he sent to publishers. We all know—as did Beethoven—that musical notation is imperfect, but it is the closest representation we have to the artistic ideal of a composer. We strive to represent that ideal as thoroughly and accurately as possible.

Tempo

My recordings of these sonatas are available as companions to the two published volumes. I have also included my suggestions for tempo (metronome markings) for each sonata, at the beginning of each movement.

Fingering

I have included Beethoven's own fingering suggestions. His fingerings—intended not only for himself (in earlier sonatas) but primarily for successive generations of pianists—often reveal intensely musical intentions in their shaping of musical contour and molding of the hands to create specific musical textures. I have added my own fingering suggestions, all of which are aimed at creating meaningful musical constructs. As a general guide, I believe in minimizing hand motions as much as possible, and therefore many of my fingering suggestions are based on the pianist's hands proceeding in a straight line as long as musically viable and physically practicable. I also believe that the pianist can develop senses of tactile feeling for specific musical patterns.

Pedaling

I have also included Beethoven's pedal markings in this edition. These indications are integral parts of the musical fabric. However, since most often no pedal indication is offered, whenever necessary one should use the right pedal—sparingly and subtly—to help achieve legato playing as well as to enhance sonorities.

Ornamentation

My suggestions regarding ornamental turns concern the notion of keeping the contour smooth while providing an expressive musical gesture with an increased sense of forward direction. The actual starting note of a turn depends on the specific context: if it is preceded by the same note (as in Sonata Op. 10 no. 2, second movement, m. 42), then I would suggest that the turn is four notes, starting on the upper neighbor: upper neighbor, main note, lower neighbor, main note.

Sonata in F Major, Opus 10 no. 2:
second movement, m. 42, r.h.

However, if the turn is preceded by another note (as in Sonata Op. 10 no. 2, first movement, m. 38), then the turn could be five notes in total, starting on the main note: main note, upper neighbor, main note, lower neighbor, main note.

Sonata in F Major, Opus 10 no. 2:
first movement, m. 38, r.h.

Whenever Beethoven included an afterbeat (Nachschlag) for a trill, I have included it as well. When he did not, I have not added any.

Footnotes

Footnotes within the musical score offer contextual explanations and alternatives based on earlier representations of the music (first editions, autograph scores) that Beethoven had seen and corrected. In areas where specific markings are visible only in the autograph score, I explain the reasons and context for my choices of musical representation. Other footnotes are intended to clarify ways of playing specific ornaments.

Notes on the Sonata[1]

PIANO SONATA NO. 2 IN A MAJOR, OPUS 2 NO. 2 (1795)

Sonata in A major, Op. 2 no. 2, is a gentle and graceful work, the most playful of the three in this opus.

From the beginning of the opening **Allegro vivace**, I use a light touch and clear articulation (well-rounded fingers!) as the opening interval (A–E) is manipulated to motivate the entire first theme area. The swirling counterpoint gives the impression of frisky new voices constantly being added, and the tempo can be quick enough to give a sense of urgent direction to the ascending lines, for the sixteenth and thirty-second note figures are not difficult to play fast. However, the *espressivo* marking in mm. 58–59 implies a lessening of tempo as well as a deeper quality of sound and touch.

Contrasts in touch help convey the differences in feeling between the first and second theme areas. Whereas the lines of the first theme area are tossed back and forth playfully between the two hands, the second theme, a single melodic line in the treble area, has a heavier, singing tone. The left hand accompanies and can play more lightly than the right, increasing in intensity as it ascends. Since I take Beethoven's fingering indications in the cascading octave triplet arpeggios (mm. 84–89) to indicate a smoothness of line as well as a display of brilliant virtuosity, I make sure not to rush the tempo in these measures and in those immediately preceding.

The characterization of the slow movement of Sonata Op. 2 no. 2—**Largo appassionato**—is highly individual. Usually passion is associated with faster music, but here the slow and dignified music is of an ardor sincere and ingenuous. The detached bass is the line with the greatest amount of motion. The long, sustained right-hand chords in this movement stand in great contrast to the rapid motion of the top line of the first movement, and playing them with a weighty touch and a sense of solemnity helps create the quiet but impassioned mood. Throughout the movement,

whenever the opening music is heard, the right hand is marked *tenuto sempre*, the left, *staccato sempre*. Yet even within these indications, there are enormous contrasts of touch and sound: consider the *fortissimo* D minor area in m. 58 and the *pianissimo* recurrence of D major in a higher octave in m. 68. The prolongation of the final cadence is again analogous to a long goodbye in Italian opera; a little extra emphasis on the low left-hand A's, prolonging the six-four chord, heightens this feeling.

The reworking of the A–E interval that so motivated the first movement also helps to make the **Scherzo: Allegretto** frolicsome. Now it is heard only in arpeggiated fragments, ascending, played almost in an off-the-cuff manner. The longer lines of the Trio provide contrast, as does the minor mode, and the *sforzando* markings highlight the entrances of new implied voices.

In the **Rondo: Grazioso**, the same A–E interval is expanded over a two-and-a-half-octave span. It would have been far easier for Beethoven to write simply two eighth notes at the end of the first beat of m. 2 (and in analogous places), but instead, the sixteenth rest following the sixteenth note implies a lift, a breath, helping significantly to establish the graceful disposition of the movement. Whenever the theme recurs, the arpeggio is slightly different, but a sixteenth rest always follows.

Contrasting with the smoothness and elegance of the first part of the Rondo, the middle section starts *fortissimo*, with staccato chromatic lines accompanying forceful dotted rhythms. The music drives forward; even when the lines are legato, *pianissimo*, and back in a major mode (m. 80 on) there is an underlying restlessness that is relieved only with the return in m. 100 of the main thematic A–E interval, now fully extended over three-and-a-half octaves! Quick changes of mood, touch, and tone color are needed in the coda of this movement (beginning in m. 148) to create a microcosm in which the principal nature of each theme resurfaces.

1 Excerpted from *Playing the Beethoven Piano Sonatas* by Robert Taub
  edited and abridged by Susanne Sheston
  © 2002 by Robert Taub
  Published by Amadeus Press
  Used by permission.

Dedicated to Joseph Haydn

Sonata in A Major

Ludwig van Beethoven
Opus 2 no. 2
Composed in 1795

Allegro vivace ($\downarrow$ = 138)

a) The fingering in italics is Beethoven's.

b) The first edition (Artaria, 1796) has ∿; the Berlin edition (Lischke, 1797), ∿.

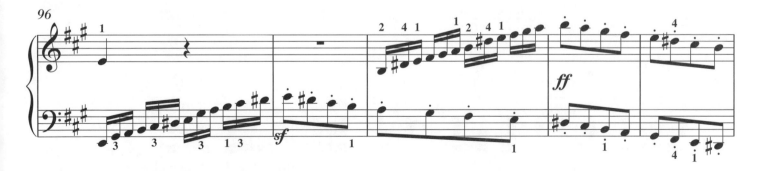

c) In Artaria,♮; in Lischke,♯. d) In Artaria and Lischke,♯. e) Beethoven's fingering here (and in parallel passages), although challenging, is purposefully integral to
the musical fabric, creating a smooth musical line as a transition back to the opening tempo from the subtly slightly slower second theme. An often-cited alternative method
of playing this passage—using the LH to play the first of each three-note group—is superficially easier, but often creates a pointillistic bravura display that countermands
the musical value.

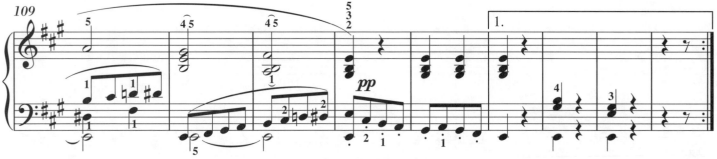

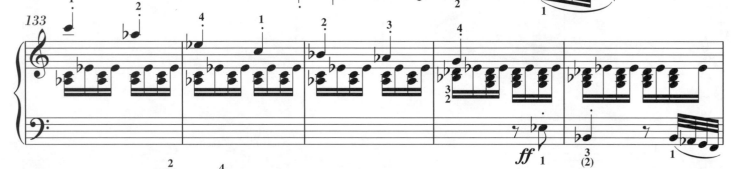

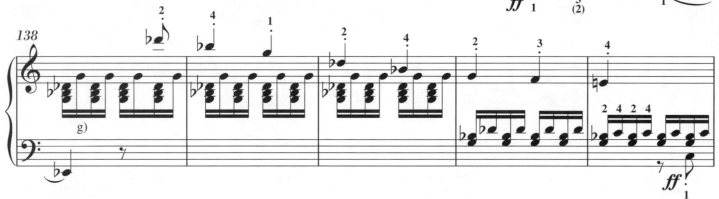

f) LH over RH g) After Artaria and Lischke, other editions print E-flat instead of G.

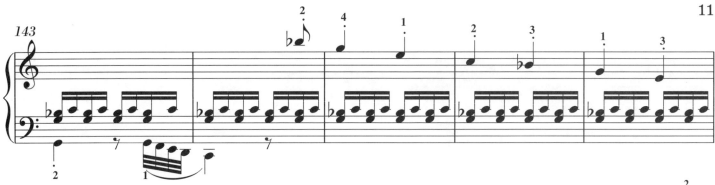

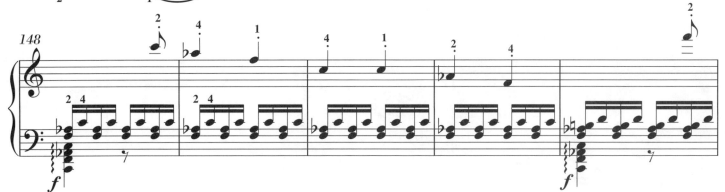

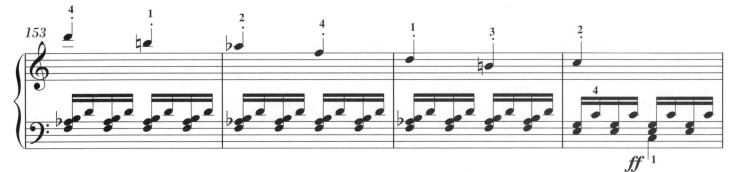

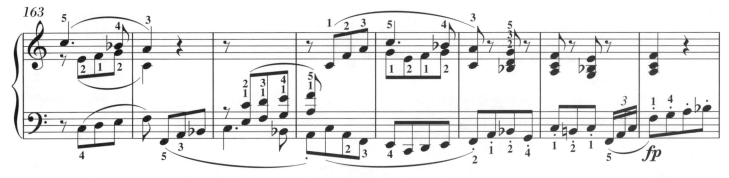

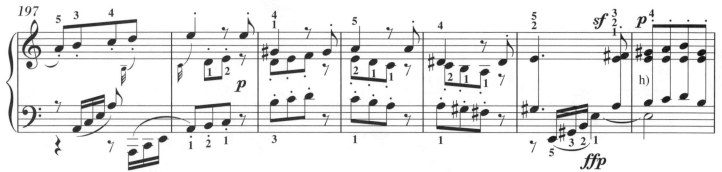

h) In m. 203, Artaria and Lischke have four G-sharps in the upper voice. Later editions have what is printed here. This change, which parallels m. 207, may be assumed to
   be the result of a correction to the first edition made by Beethoven.

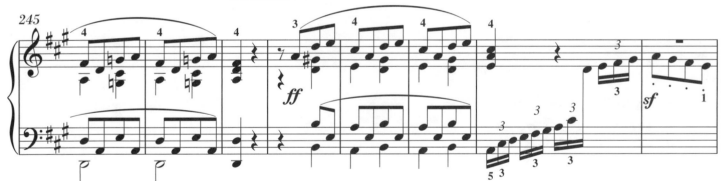

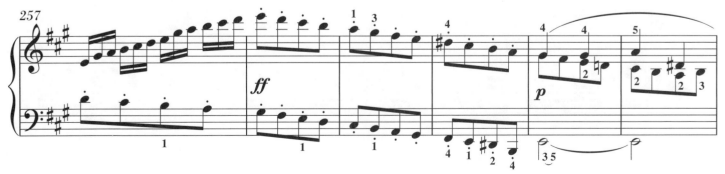

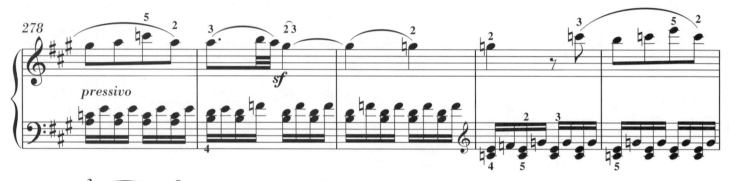

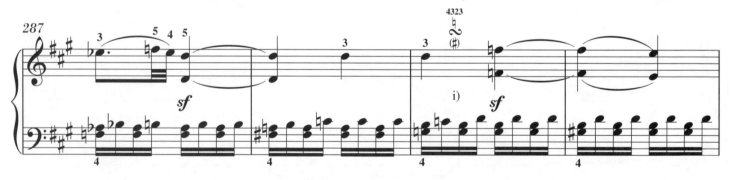

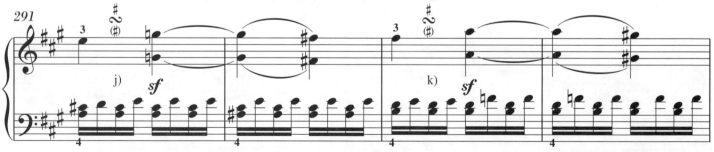

i) In Artaria and Lischke, 𝄍. j) In Artaria and Lischke, 𝄍. k) In Artaria and Lischke, 𝄍.

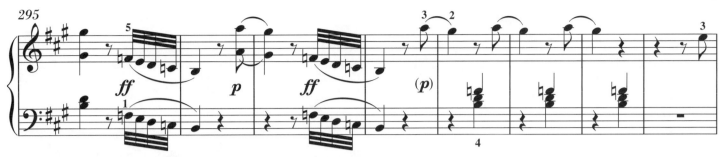

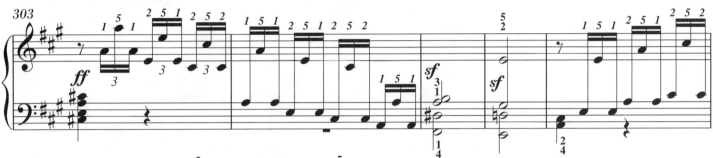

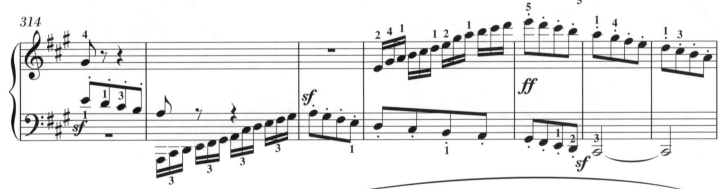

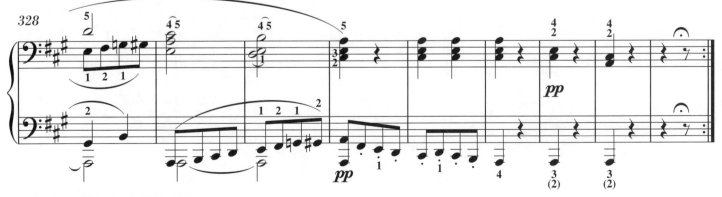

l) In both first editions, only E–B in LH.

Largo appassionato (♪ = 66)

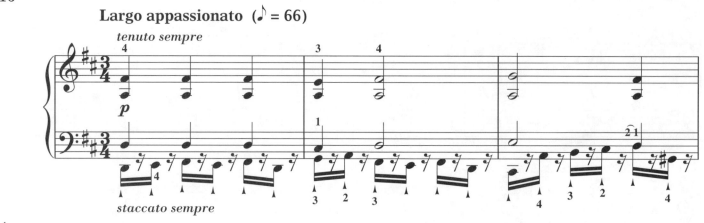

m) For the sake of "languid expression" (C.P.E. Bach), the turn may begin on the second eighth note. n) The trill begins with the principal note.

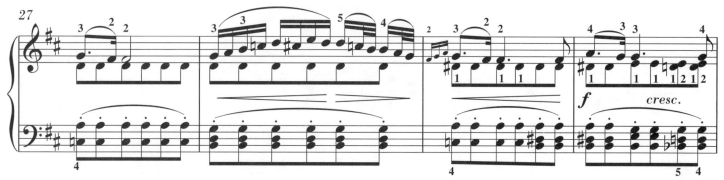

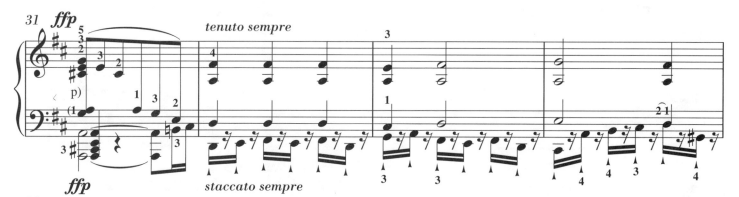

o) p) Notation of LH follows Artaria. Lischke prints and some more recent editions print

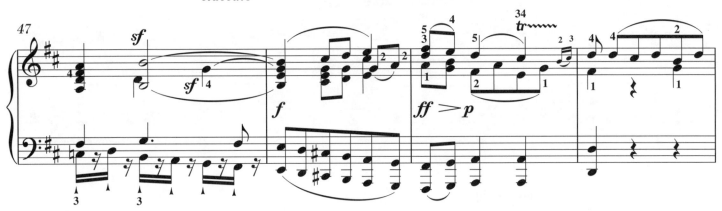

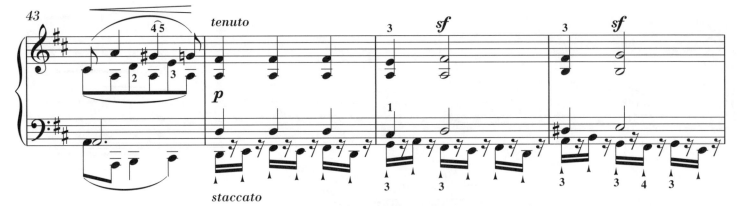

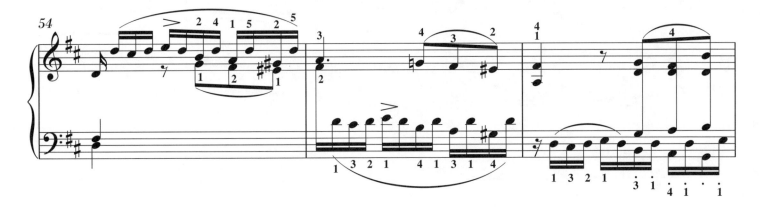

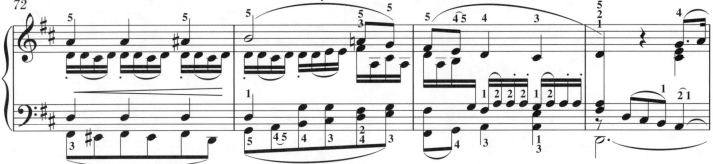

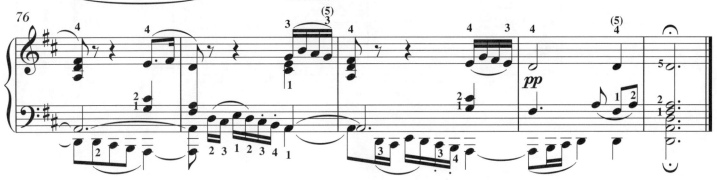

SCHERZO
Allegretto (♩ = 168)

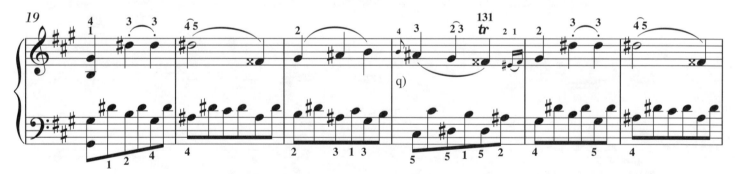

q) Expressive short appoggiatura:

Scherzo D.C.

r) **ff**, as in Artasia; in Lischke, the **ff** is one measure later.

RONDO
Grazioso (♩ = 120)

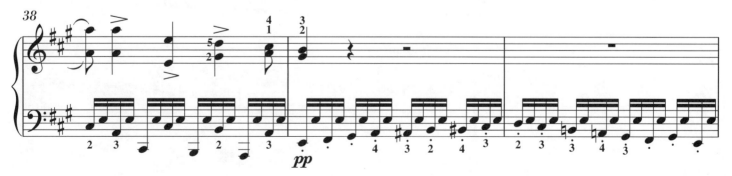

staccato sempre

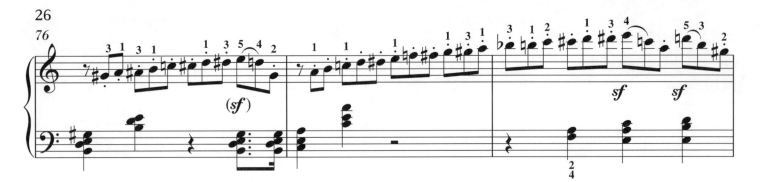

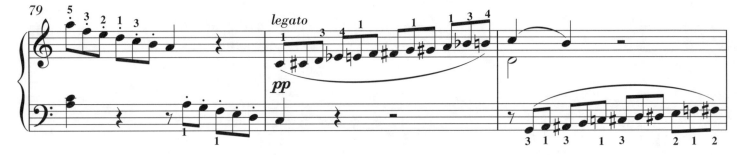

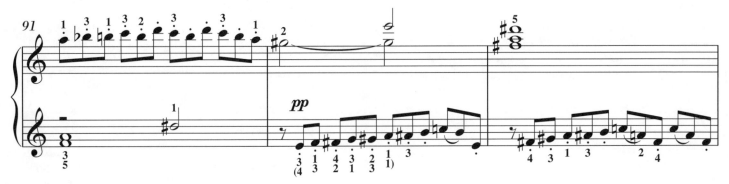

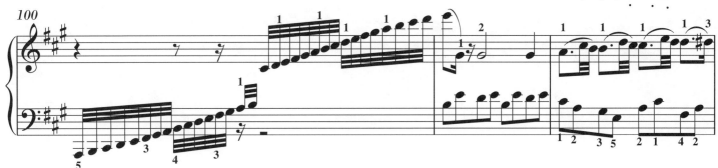

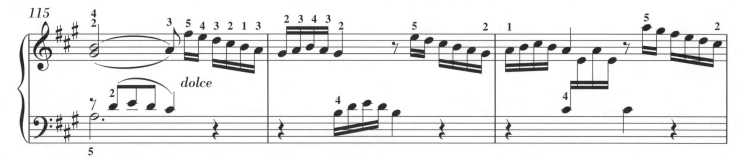

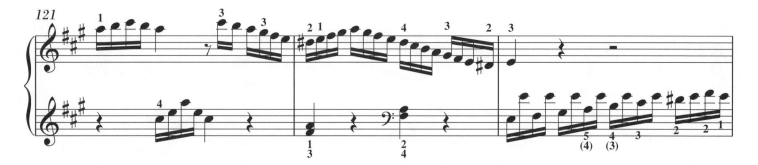

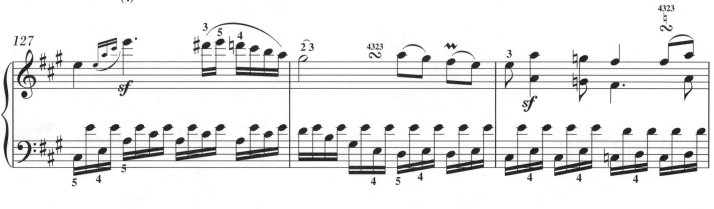

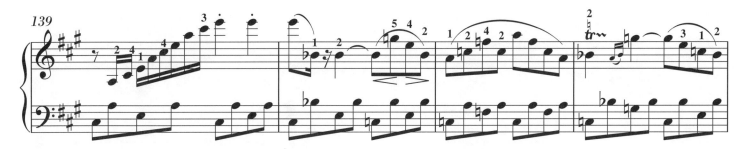

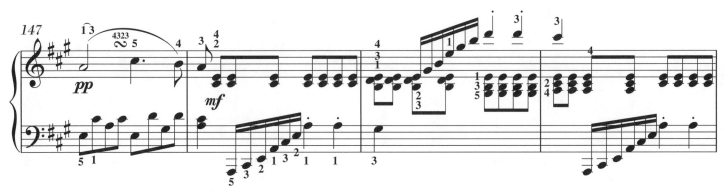

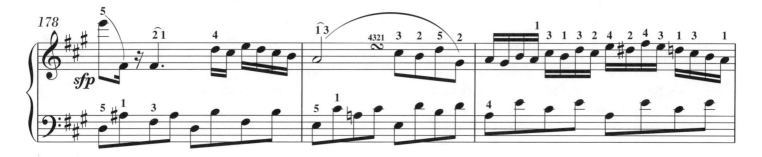

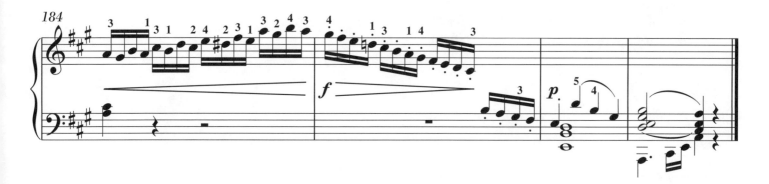

ABOUT THE EDITOR

ROBERT TAUB

From New York's Carnegie Hall to Hong Kong's Cultural Centre to Germany's *avant garde* Zentrum für Kunst und Medientechnologie, Robert Taub is acclaimed internationally. He has performed as soloist with the MET Orchestra in Carnegie Hall, the Boston Symphony Orchestra, BBC Philharmonic, The Philadelphia Orchestra, San Francisco Symphony, Los Angeles Philharmonic, Montreal Symphony, Munich Philharmonic, Orchestra of St. Luke's, Hong Kong Philharmonic, Singapore Symphony, and others.

Robert Taub has performed solo recitals on the Great Performers Series at New York's Lincoln Center and other major series worldwide. He has been featured in international festivals, including the Saratoga Festival, the Lichfield Festival in England, San Francisco's Midsummer Mozart Festival, the Geneva International Summer Festival, among others.

Following the conclusion of his highly celebrated New York series of Beethoven Piano Sonatas, Taub completed a sold-out Beethoven cycle in London at Hampton Court Palace. His recordings of the complete Beethoven Piano Sonatas have been praised throughout the world for their insight, freshness, and emotional involvement. In addition to performing, Robert Taub is an eloquent spokesman for music, giving frequent engaging and informal lectures and pre-concert talks. His book on Beethoven—*Playing the Beethoven Piano Sonatas*—has been published internationally by Amadeus Press.

Taub was featured in a recent PBS television program—*Big Ideas*—that highlighted him playing and discussing Beethoven Piano Sonatas. Filmed during his time as Artist-in-Residence at the Institute for Advanced Study, this program has been broadcast throughout the US on PBS affiliates.

Robert Taub's performances are frequently broadcast on radio networks around the world, including the NPR (Performance Today), Ireland's RTE, and Hong Kong's RTHK. He has also recorded the Sonatas of Scriabin and works of Beethoven, Schumann, Liszt, and Babbitt for Harmonia Mundi, several of which have been selected as "critic's favorites" by *Gramophone*, *Newsweek*, *The New York Times*, *The Washington Post*, *Ovation*, and *Fanfare*.

Robert Taub is involved with contemporary music as well as the established literature, premiering piano concertos by Milton Babbitt (MET Orchestra, James Levine) and Mel Powell (Los Angeles Philharmonic), and making the first recordings of the Persichetti Piano Concerto (Philadelphia Orchestra, Charles Dutoit) and Sessions Piano Concerto. He has premiered six works of Milton Babbitt (solo piano, chamber music, Second Piano Concerto). Taub has also collaborated with several 21st-century composers, including Jonathan Dawe (USA), David Bessell (UK), and Ludger Brümmer (Germany) performing their works in America and Europe.

Taub is a Phi Beta Kappa graduate of Princeton where he was a University Scholar. As a Danforth Fellow he completed his doctoral degree at The Juilliard School where he received the highest award in piano. Taub has served as Artist-in-Residence at Harvard University, at UC Davis, as well as at the Institute for Advanced Study. He has led music forums at Oxford and Cambridge Universities and The Juilliard School. Taub has also been Visiting Professor at Princeton University and at Kingston University (UK).